T0209967

Bent But Not Broken

PATRICIA CLARKE ROLLE

WESTBOW
PRESS®
A DIVISION OF THOMAS NELSON
& ZONDERVAN

WestBow Press books may be ordered through booksellers or by contacting:

WestBow Press
A Division of Thomas Nelson & Zondervan
1663 Liberty Drive
Bloomington, IN 47403
www.westbowpress.com
844-714-3454

ISBN: 978-1-6642-8399-2 (sc)
ISBN: 978-1-6642-8400-5 (e)

Library of Congress Control Number: 2022921198

Print information available on the last page.

WestBow Press rev. date: 1/31/2023

Acknowledgements

I thought writing sermons was difficult but writing a book is much more complicated and detailed. Firstly, if the lights go off while preaching a sermon, one can improvise by speaking from memory or stop preaching; but not so with a book that someone is reading. Secondly, a sermon has no direct feedback to say whether all your **T**s were crossed or whether your **I**s were dotted. You are the only one who may get to read your sermon and critique it. I also found out that writing a book takes the support of some special people. So let me say thanks to all those who made this book happen, by way of support, advice, encouragement, inspiration and editing.

I have to start by thanking Almighty God for his unmerited favor towards me, in allowing me to accomplish one of my goals in writing and publishing my first book.

I would also like to thank my family. Especially my amazing husband, Avery. For his encouragement and support when I stayed up late at nights doing research. His patience and timely word of advice was very important to get this book done. Thank you so much my dear. To my daughter, Averia. For being the scribe, my constant reminder of deadlines and for giving her honest opinion. Thank you, my dear daughter, for flagging me and reminding not to give up. I really appreciate you and your dedication.

To my son, Cardell J. McClam (sonny boy, Cardellicious). You were my number one consistent and persistence motivator. You never stop telling me that I could do it. You believed in my talent and ability to write and complete this book. Thank you, 'Sonny Boy', for every phone call; every word of encouragement, thank you Cardell for your input and critique of this book. Your persistence was one of the stabling influences that caused me to complete this book.

To Mr. Paul K. Ellis Jr.. You sir was the catalyst, the icing on the cake, and the rude awakening to put this budding writer on the right track. Our startling encounter and your timely seminars for Fledging Writer's held in Florida, awaken the sleeping giant within me. Every speaker, and every session caused my creative inner being to come alive. Thank you, sir. You were the first to critique this book; when you were through with your corrections and timely input I wanted to throw in the towel, but I held on to my dreams of one day reaching this goal. Once again thank you for taking time out of your busy schedule to assist.

A special thank you to my spiritual sons and daughters in the Bahamas, Turks & Caicos Islands, and around the globe for your support and encouragement. Special mention must be of my friends and mentees Dr. Angela Terry Brooks(my Lawyer) and Mrs. Zalmunna Dickenson(my Accountant), you ladies have inspired me with your testimonies of being bent but not Broken and you are now standing tall, thank you.

To the entire staff of Westbow Publishing Company this could not happen with you. Thank you for returning every phone call and answering when I called with my concerns. Thanks for your patience and timely guidance while I navigated through those beginner's moments. Most of all thank you for affirming and believing that my book was worthwhile publishing.

Finally, thanks to my readers for reading **Bent but not Broken.** May you be inspired and motivated to stand up straight, after reading this book. Thanks for sharing this book with your family and friends. Many blessings on your life.

Contents

Introduction...ix

Chapter 1 Perspective of the Bent Over Giants, Milk, Honey, Grapes,
and Grasshoppers...1

Chapter 2 My Story, Your Story, Our Story!................................6

Chapter 3 The World Viewed from the Ground Up.....................13

Chapter 4 The Abrahamic Covenant...16

Chapter 5 Hope That Makes Us Not Ashamed 19

Chapter 6 Positioned for a Miracle 23

Chapter 7 Stand Up and Praise..28

Conclusion...33

About the Author..35

Introduction

If you have ever twisted your ankle, do you recall the moment when the pain started and spread to your entire foot? Did it hurt to the point that massaging it was not sufficient to ease the pain? At that point, you realized that you would need more than a cold or a hot pack; you needed professional medical assistance if only to understand and monitor the pain. One day's mishap would transcend into a tenure of medical attention.

Were you ever punched in the stomach and fell over due to its excruciating pain? The punch left you winded; you were breathless, and you could not lift yourself up.

Have you ever been hurt so badly that you felt you would not survive? Has your character and your name been pulled through the ringer in the most vicious and evil ways by those who were supposed to have your back?

While he was running and hiding from Saul, King David expressed his hurt and betrayal in Psalm 55:12-13 (KJV).

> For it was not an enemy that reproached me; then I could have borne it: neither was it he that hated me that did magnify himself against me; then I would have hid myself from him: But it was thou, a man mine equal, my guide, and mine acquaintance.

You may have experienced the loss of a loved one, a divorce, suicidal thoughts, a broken heart, a physical ailment that left you all bent and out of shape. Then the coming of old age and being single has caused you to wonder if God has somehow forgotten you. You may feel that you cannot take the scrutiny of the crowd that passes your way, and you have been lonely and afraid. Your circumstances and life's trials have jaded your view of whether you can face tomorrow with confidence. Depression and phobias have magnified and distorted your view of what could have been the brighter side of life.

Well, if you have read so far, this book is just for you! If your perspective on life has been bent and distorted due to life's difficult lessons, I declare that you are not beyond help. I invite you to declare with me, "I might be bent, but I'm not broken!" And repeat, as necessary.

CHAPTER 1

Perspective of the Bent Over Giants, Milk, Honey, Grapes, and Grasshoppers

> "In case you have fallen by the wayside of life, dreams and visions shattered you're all broken inside, you do not have to stay in the shape that you're in, the Potter wants to put you back together again."
> —Tremaine Hawkins

Merriam Webster's defines the word *perspective* as "2a. the interrelation in which a subject or its parts are mentally viewed: places the issues in proper perspective; also: point of view, and b. the capacity to view things in their true relations or relative importance."

God does not view human fragility as we do. His perspective on our situation is different from ours: "For my thoughts are not your thoughts, nor are your ways My ways," says the Lord' (Isaiah 55:8 NKJV). How you view your circumstances determines your attitude and outcome.

1 Samuel 17:44-47 tells us that when King David was a teenager, he killed a giant named Goliath. David never paid attention to the size of the giant; his focus was on the 'bigness' of his God. Whereas Goliath presumed that David's perspective of him was, Am I a dog? What do you do with wild dogs? You give their head to the fowls of the air. (Take note that it was Goliath who likened himself to a dog, not David). How you perceive yourself to be will make you careless and presumptuous. Do not be like Goliath and think you have certain bragging rights over the enemy in your own strength and power. "It's not by might, nor by power, but by my Spirit,' says the Lord of hosts" (Zechariah 4:1 KJV). You and I can conquer giants only in the name of the Lord of hosts.

Never underestimate the power of belief. If you perceive yourself to be a nobody, you will inherently begin to believe that and act that way. Low self-esteem will have you believing that you deserve to be living a defeated life and that a bent-over life is what God has planned for you. Declare now: "I will not tolerate giants to challenge my well-being another day. Giants of fear, low self-esteem, and hopelessness, die now in the name of Jesus" [Cut his head off with the sword of the Spirit, which is the Word of God] (Ephesians 17 NKJV).

Scripture declares: But what saith it? The word is nigh thee, even in thy mouth, and in thy heart: that is, the word of faith, which we preach. Romans 10:8 KJV It is important to know the word of God. Hebrews 4:12 (NIV) tells us, "For the word of God is alive and active. Sharper than any double-edged sword." While David's weapon was a slingshot, ours is the Bible, which gives us the power to crush the enemy and make him powerless in the name of Jesus.

In Numbers 12:1–15 (KJV), Aaron and Miriam, Moses's siblings, assumed that Moses was an ordinary man like them. Verse 2 states, "And they said, 'hath the Lord indeed spoken only by Moses? Hath he not spoken also by us?' And the Lord heard." It is important that God's chosen leadership received respect and were viewed as God's mouthpieces because when we speak out against them, God will hear and act. Do not allow your negative perspective of leadership to dim your view of their relationship with God.

Numbers 13:27–33 (NIV) expresses one of most profound and yet sad thought processes of a bent-over feeling of self and self-worth. One must be careful who is placed in a leadership position, it could either make or break the group. Observe Moses's leadership team; most of his leadership team in verses 27-29 and 31-33, did not believe in themselves nor in their ability to conquer the Promise land.

> They gave Moses this account: "We went into the land to which you sent us, and it does flow with milk and honey! Here is its fruit. But the people who live there are powerful, and the cities are fortified and very large. We even saw descendants of Anak there. The Amalekites live in the Negev; the Hittites, Jebusites and Amorites live in the hill country; and the Canaanites live near the sea and along the Jordan." Numbers 13:27-29(NIV)

> Then Caleb silenced the people before Moses and said, "We should go up and take possession of the land, for we can certainly do it."

> But the men who had gone up with him said, "We can't attack those people; they are stronger than we are." And they spread among the Israelites a bad report about the land they had explored. They said, "The land we explored devours those living in it. All the people we saw there are of great size.(giants) We saw the Nephilim there (the descendants of Anak come from the Nephilim). We seemed like grasshoppers in our own eyes, and we looked the same to them." Numbers 13:30-33.

What do giants, milk, honey, grapes, and grasshoppers have in common? What do you imagine when you think about those things? Do you see giants drinking milk, eating honey and grapes, and crushing grasshoppers?

Ten of the men sent to spy on the land returned with an evil report as perhaps a fearful person would. The Israelites' perspective on the report that they heard was negative, and they reacted in fear. They saw the giants drinking the milk and eating the honey and grapes, and they saw themselves as grasshoppers crushed by the giants in the land. How do you see yourself in view of your circumstances?

Hundreds of years before the report of milk, honey, grapes, and grasshoppers, God made a promise to Abraham that he would give his descendants a fertile land. God made a covenant with Abraham hundreds of years before the spies went out: "And the Lord appeared unto Abram, and said, unto thy seed will I give this land: and there built him an altar unto the Lord, who appeared unto him." (Genesis 12:7 KJV) When you have the legal right to a piece of land, it does not matter who or what is on it; it is your land because you have the paper for it. If God makes a promised to you whether prophetically or in a word of knowledge, you have the legal authority to own it, build on it, live on it, and eat of it. It is yours! Declare it with me: "It is my inheritance!"

Moses sent twelve leaders to view the land that the children of Israel were to have. He wanted his leadership team's opinion on its potential, but ten of them magnified their fear instead of their faith. Pastors, managers, and those heading organizations, be careful of whom you surround yourself with. Their view of the situation is at times clouded by their fear and negative experiences. Their negative report will influence others and eventually sabotage your God-given vision as the ten spies did with Moses. Those ten along with Moses never experienced the covenanted promise land.

A bent-over attitude could be the result of hurt, pain, anger, bitterness, and low self-esteem handed down from generation to generation in the form of unresolved family issues involving deviant behavior, bad attitudes, and poor dispositions for instance. Sicknesses and diseases have been known to perpetuate through the genes of certain families. Noncommunicable diseases such as diabetes, hypertension, heart conditions, cancer, and other ailments such as mental illness are sometimes passed on genetically. Are you struggling with anything generational that you have no control over? Or are you holding onto something that affected you negatively? You do not have to accept it; you can be free from it.

What has you bent over and out of shape? What has clouded your judgment so that you cannot make clear, concise, and right decisions? What has you so bent over and out of shape that you cannot lift yourself up? You have been carrying it around for years. God wants to heal everywhere you hurt. Jesus said, "Come to me, all you who are weary and burdened, and I will give you rest" (Matthew 11:28 NIV).

When your attitude and disposition in life is negative (bent over), the joy you get from new insights is different from that experienced by people whose situations might be negative but who have found peace in having the right perspective on life. In Mark 8:24 (NIV), we read, "Jesus touched a blind man eye to heal him, Jesus then asked him, 'what do you see?' the blind man replied, 'I see people; they look like trees walking around.' That is how we oftentimes view our circumstances. Things may look blurry now, but I command your eyes to come open so that you see clearly in Jesus's name. See by faith that things are already better; it has not changed yet, but your perspective is changing. Your outlook is clearer. Let Jesus touch your eyes again as he did with the blind man. Ask God to open your spiritual eyes so that you may see that there is more with you than those who are against you.

CHAPTER 2

My Story, Your Story, Our Story!

Luke 13:10–17 (NIV) tells the story of a nameless and faceless woman. Her story is our story, the story of the fallen human race.

> On a Sabbath Jesus was teaching in one of the synagogues, and a woman was there who had been crippled by a spirit for eighteen years. She was bent over and could not straighten up at all. When Jesus saw her, he called her forward and said to her, "Woman, you are set free from your infirmity." Then he put his hand on her, and at once she straightened up and praised God.

> Indignant because Jesus had healed on the Sabbath, the synagogue leader said to the people, "There are six days for work. So be healed on those days, not on the Sabbath."

> The Lord answered him, "You hypocrites! Doesn't each of you on the Sabbath untie your ox or donkey from the stall and lead it out to give it water? Then should not this woman, a daughter of Abraham,

whom Satan has kept bound for eighteen long years, be set free on the Sabbath day from what bound her?"

When he said this, all his opponents were humiliated, but the people were delighted with all the wonderful things he was doing.

Can you imagine going to church for eighteen years bent over with arthritis or another debilitating disease? The Bible said that she "could not lift herself up." She was helpless; she could not heal herself, and it was impossible for her to look anyone in the face because she was so bent over. Just walking for her was a task.

Are you in that predicament physically or spiritually? Jesus is there now in your room, at your desk, on the plane, by your bedside—wherever you are or whatever position you are in. He is saying to you, "Stand up straight." Receive healing in your body, mind, and emotions.

At some point and time in everyone's life we have a story to tell of being bent over in pain, disappointment, the sudden death of a loved one, etc. So many stories of failure, persecution, rejection, fear and of abandonment even while sitting a church pew.

This faceless woman had attended the synagogue for eighteen years, yet no one knew her name. No other gospel mentions her name; she was known only as the bent-over woman who had a "spirit of infirmity." No one paid attention to her. Others thought her disease was demonic and did not want to touch her, and according to Jewish custom then, women were to a degree lesser men. She was to be in the background and not seen or heard. The odds of this woman being set free were nil.

Jewish Women and the Temple

In the Temple proper the females occupied, according to Jewish tradition, only a raised gallery along three sides of the court. They were allowed to observe the ceremonies but never to participate in them.

Rabbinic literature was filled with contempt for women. The rabbis taught that women were not to be greeted, or spoken to in the street, and they were not to be instructed in the law or receive an inheritance. A woman walked six paces behind her husband and if she uncovered her hair in a public place, she was considered a harlot.

Women in the First Century A.D.

In ancient Israel, the Jewish culture was one of the most male dominant cultures in the entire world. In ancient Judaism the woman only had rights in the home and even that was extremely limited. The man had authority over his wife and daughters setting up their activities and their relationships. Women were passed from the control of her father to the control of her husband with little or no say in the matter. They were usually sold for a dowry settlement when they came of age. The Mishnah taught that a woman was like a gentile slave who could be obtained by intercourse, money, or writ (m. Qidd 1:1).

Women could not play a significant role in the synagogue because they were levitically unclean for several days every month during their menstrual cycle. Women were not even counted as members in a synagogue count. They did not recite the daily shema, they did not read the Torah in the synagogue (Ber 3:3), they were not required to come to any feasts or festivals, and the Mishnah says: "The observance of all the positive ordinances that depend on the time of year is incumbent on men but not on women."

Women were only allowed to receive little education on religion and the main religious instruction in the home was given by the man and not the woman. They could not be disciples of any great rabbi; they certainly could not travel with any rabbi.

In court a woman's testimony was considered suspect (m. Ned. 11:10). Women also did not have the right to divorce.

[1] Bible-history.com

Jesus the Radical

Considering what we know about Jewish life in the first century A.D. Jesus' teaching must have seemed very radical. He was not one to show partiality. In fact, women followed Jesus... including prostitutes. Scripture mention names of some of the women who followed Jesus such as: Mary Magdalene, Mary the mother of James and Joseph, the "other Mary" the mother of the sons of Zebedee, and of course Mary and Martha. Jesus was genuinely concerned with the treatment of women, and in fact a great part of His ministry was in direct relationship with women. One of the first people that Jesus healed was Peter's mother (Mark 1). Jesus also healed the woman with the hemorrhage (Luke 8), He raised the widow of Nain's son from the dead (Luke 7), He healed the Syro-Phoenician woman's daughter (Mark 7), and when Mary and Martha pleaded with Him, He raised Lazarus from the dead (John 11).

[1]   Bible-history.com

In Jesus' teachings He focused on women quite often and used women as illustrations of spiritual truths in His teachings. One woman loses a coin (Luke 15), two women are grinding at the mill just before His return in glory (Luke 17). On his journey to Galilee, He passed through Samaria and comes to Jacob's well at Sychar and ministers to a woman of questionable reputation (John 4). Jesus also ministered to the woman caught in adultery (John 7). Notice that women followed Jesus from Galilee to Jerusalem: Matt 27:55-56"NKJ "And many women who followed Jesus from Galilee, ministering to Him, were there looking on from afar, among whom were Mary Magdalene, Mary the mother of James and Joses, and the mother of Zebedee's sons."

And these women were there at His crucifixion. After Jesus was crucified, the women prepared His body for burial with spices and ointments (Matt 27).

On the morning of the resurrection the women were the first to the tomb and the first to see the risen Lord (Matt 28).

After Jesus rose from the dead and ascended into heaven, He commissioned His apostles and breathed the Holy Spirit into them. As the 120 were waiting in the Upper Room in Jerusalem there is mention "the women" Acts 1:14 NKJV.

Acts 1:14 NKV, "These all continued with one accord in prayer and supplication, with the women and Mary the mother of Jesus, and with His brothers. "Jesus showed no partiality to men even in the fact that He chose twelve male apostles. In Christ women are liberated to serve Jesus in an equal manner.

Galatians 3:28 NIV "There is neither Jew nor Greek, there is neither slave nor free, there is neither male nor female; for you are all one in Christ Jesus."

[2]Bible-history.com

Today, Jesus is still elevating men and women from whatever has them bent over. He is laying his hand on you by faith and commanding you to stand up straight. It is your time to face the future with confidence and say to the enemy, "Jesus laid his hand on me, and I am giving him praise and glory. I am no longer bound. I am free!"

The odds were against that woman. Her infirmity was physical, but she also suffered from a psychological burden. Years of living emotionally bent over can leave one bitter, empty, and almost lifeless. How people treated you, and the harsh words spoken about you may have left you emotionally and mentally drained and almost ready to give up, but you should square your shoulders and hold your head up because your situation is about to change. Your view of yourself changes as you begin to realize that what you went through was only a process.

Jesus is visiting you right now. He is in your room, by your hospital bed, and he is walking with you through the valley of shadow of death. He is seeking the wounded, the bruised, the overlooked, the lonely, the brokenhearted, and the bent over. He has come to look for and save those who are lost and lift those who cannot lift themselves up.

---

[2]

He is beckoning you to come forth and stand up. Let him touch you; let him heal your brokenness. Allow his touch to revolutionize your view of your situation. Your story can change today! With just one touch of the master's hand, your life will never be the same.

CHAPTER 3

The World Viewed from the Ground Up

Imagine being bent over and all you can see is the ground. Imagine that that has been your condition for eighteen long years. Your view of the world would be of dusty feet and dirty sandals. The bent-over woman made her own path to the synagogue. Her view at ground level was dim and full of dust. She knew every pebble and the root of every tree on her way to the synagogue. When you are staring down, your view of the world is narrow and different from those who can see the color of houses, the faces of the people they pass, and the flowers in gardens.

A crowd must have been one of her greatest fears because of the danger of being trampled. Do you have a phobia that you struggle with daily? There is a Savior who wants to deliver you from every fear you have such as the fear of dying, flying, failing, heights, public speaking, and of looking your fearful situations in the face and commanding them to get behind you.

In 1 John 4:18, we read, "Perfect love cast out fear," and 2 Timothy 1:7 (KJV) tells us, "God has not given us a spirit of fear, but of love and of a sound mind." We can walk on those fears today. Peter, one of Jesus's disciples, did so. He walked on the billowing waves in the middle of a storm. Jesus bade Peter to walk on turbulent waves. My brother, my sister, sometimes Jesus calls us to walk with him on the tempestuous seas of life's most tricky situations. Keep your eyes on him, and he will see you safely through. Do not be afraid; obey his voice and trust his plans for your life. You can stand up and stand up straight.

The bent-over woman in Luke 13:10–17 must have had other burdens that weighed heavily on her mind. An emotional as well as a spiritual expectation of healing kept her going back to the synagogue. I wonder if the other women at the synagogue talked to her. Did they add her to their women's group, their inner circle? Did people care enough to pray for her, or was she just a lonely, desperate soul following the Judaic law of keeping the Sabbath holy and waiting expectantly for the Messiah to come? What kept her going back week after week in her bent over condition? Today's churchgoers would not go back to a church if they were offended or even if someone looked at them in a way, they thought offensive. Modern Christianity has lost its sense of commitment, dedication, and perseverance. Statistics have proven that today's Christians change churches once a year on average. They think, *I am led to move on*, or *My time is up here*, or *the pastor offended me*, or *too many hypocrites in that church*. Others think, *If the preaching does not make me feel good, I am gone*. The church hoppers are like those who start shopping at a new mall as soon as it opens and then move on to the next new mall … No stability, no waiting for the troubling of the water, no praying or fasting, no waiting on the Lord to come through.

Yet this daughter of Abraham went to the synagogue for eighteen years in faith expecting 'a move of God' that would bring healing for her body soul and spirit. What tenacity! Jesus called her a daughter of Abraham, meaning she was a woman of faith, a woman who had an inheritance of covenant healing, and she could not be denied. Healing for this bent-over woman was delayed for eighteen years, but she refused to give up. She kept on trekking to the synagogue every Sabbath, believing that one day, her faith would give way to victory.

For Jesus to have called this woman a daughter of Abraham meant that she had a relationship with God and believed the covenant spoken to Abraham hundreds of years earlier. Her faith in the Jehovah Rapha (the Lord who heals) was steadfast and did not waver. Is your story one of steadfast, unmovable faith? Have you been waiting for an answer to your prayers for healing, for that wondering child to come home or for your situation to change? No matter what your story is do not give up. Continue to praise and worship...the Lord is with you.

CHAPTER 4

The Abrahamic Covenant

A covenant is an agreement between two parties. There are two basic types of covenants: conditional and unconditional. A conditional or bilateral covenant is an agreement that is binding on both parties for its fulfillment. Both parties agree to fulfill certain conditions. If either party fails to meet their responsibilities, the covenant is broken and neither party must fulfill the expectations of the covenant. An unconditional or unilateral covenant is an agreement between two parties, but only one of the two parties must do something. Nothing is required of the other party.

The Abrahamic Covenant is an unconditional covenant. God made promises to Abraham that required nothing of Abraham. Genesis 15: 18-21 describes a part of the Abrahamic Covenant, specifically dealing with the dimensions of the land God promised to Abraham and his descendants.

The actual Abrahamic Covenant is found in Genesis 12:1-3. The ceremony recorded in Genesis 15 indicates the unconditional nature of the covenant. The only time that both parties of a covenant would pass between the pieces of animals was when the fulfillment of the covenant was dependent upon both parties keeping commitments. Concerning the significance of God alone moving between the halves of the animals, it is to be noted that it is a smoking furnace and a flaming torch, representing[3] God, not Abraham, which passed between the pieces. Such an act, it would seem, should be shared by both parties, but in this case God's solitary action is doubtless to be explained by the fact that the covenant is principally a promise by God. He binds Himself to the covenant. God caused a deep sleep to fall upon Abraham so that he would not be able to pass between the two halves of the hence, the fulfillment of the covenant fell to God alone.

The Abrahamic Covenant was for generations yet unborn, and after Jesus Christ died, the Gentiles by the blood of Jesus Christ inherited the Abrahamic covenant. Christ redeemed us from the curse of the law, having become a curse for us. "For it is written: 'Cursed is everyone who hangs on a tree'" (Galatians 3:13 NKJV) in order that in Christ Jesus, the blessing of Abraham might come to the Gentiles so that we would receive the promise of the Spirit through faith.

You and I have a legal right to be healed, delivered, and set free when we come to Jesus and repent of our sins and seeks his forgiveness. Christ's death has given us access to all the promises made to Abraham and more. Are you a child of Abraham by the new birth in Jesus? Are your sins forgiven? If your answer is yes, you are a member of the kingdom and you can have what you ask. Jesus said: "And

---

[3]   Olli Fobbs, Aggressive Faith

whatsoever ye shall ask in my name, that will I do, that the Father may be glorified in the Son. If ye ask any thing in my name, I will do it." John 14:13-14KJV

You are a joint heir with Jesus Christ, and you have the right to stand up straight in his name. If you have not yet made the decision to commit your life to him, this is a good opportunity. Recite this prayer.

"Lord Jesus, I am a sinner. I confess that you died on the cross for my sins, so please forgive me and come into my heart. I confess and repent of my sins. Come into my heart. Thank you, Jesus, for forgiving me and washing me in your blood. It is by faith that I ask this in your name, amen."

If you have prayed that prayer, you are a child of God by faith.

CHAPTER 5

Hope That Makes Us Not Ashamed

And hope does not put us to shame, because God's love has been poured out into our hearts through the Holy Spirit, who has been given to us.

—Romans 5:5 NIV

Hope is a strong feeling or expectation that something you have believed in will happen. Hebrews 11:1 (KJV) state, "Now faith is the substance of things hoped for, the evidence of things not seen." Have you been praying for a long time and hoping your situation would change? Do not lose hope, and do not give up.

Lazarus, Jesus's good friend, took sick and his sisters; Mary, and Martha, sent for Jesus to come and heal him. They waited expectantly for him, but Lazarus died and was buried. Jesus got to his friends' home four days later. Jesus the resurrection and the life showed up when Lazarus was already stunk and all hope to that grieving family seem loss. Brother, sister, when things around you look dismal and dreams are all shattered and dead, do not lose hope. Jesus can resurrect your dead or dying situation. It is not too late! My friends, it may seem that he is late, but God is never late. You may be going through a battle in your mind; in your marriage, with your children, in your finances, and sickness is in your body, but expect God to show up when you call on his name. Your miracle may have died like the Shunammite woman's child did in 2 Kings 4:8–37. Her miracle son had died, but she refused to give up hope. She placed her dead son on the man of God's bed and went to the man of God because she was expecting something supernatural to happen, that her son would live again, and she got what she expected. Hope does not make us ashamed. She declared 'all is well' even while knowing that her miracle promised son was dead. What are you expecting? What are you declaring? Proverbs 18:21 warns us that: "Death and life are in the power of the tongue, and those who love it will eat its fruit." Friend you will have what you say. "Have faith in God," Jesus answered, "Truly I tell you if anyone says to this mountain, 'Go throw yourself into the sea,' and does not doubt in their heart but believes that what they say will happen, it will be done for them." Mark 11:22-23(NIV). What are you saying? Are you saying what you are expecting? Is your hope still alive? If it is, you will not be put to shame.

For eighteen years, this woman went to the synagogue unashamedly hoping that one day would be her day. If you need a breakthrough, if you need help, do not be ashamed to do whatever it takes to get your miracle. People sometimes allow pride and their status in life to cause them to miss their miracle, like Naaman the leper in 2 Kings 5:7. The prophet told him to dip seven times in the Jordan River. The dirty water was below him. He was a commander in the army of Israel and a man of high degree, but he had leprosy and needed healing. A little Jewish girl encouraged him to obey the man of God (Elisha). Naaman's hope was in his gifts not in the God who heals. Naaman almost missed his miraculous healing. When he eventually got over his bent-over attitude, he received his healing.

If you want to receive something from God, it may take dipping in some dirty water seven times, it may take some spit and dirt put on your eyes, it may take going to the same place of worship with a withered hand for years, it may take waiting by a pool for thirty-eight years, but friend, Jesus has heard your cry and has seen your tears, so don't give up. He is on his way! In fact, when you call, he will answer, and while you are speaking, he will say, "Here I am."

God has not forgotten you. You may have prayed for a turnaround in your marriage, business, family, or ministry. Well, my dear sisters and brothers, praise is the breeding ground for the miraculous. He will meet you at your point of need. I decree and declare that you are stepping out of despair into your destiny. Things will not always be like this. A new day is dawning for you; that bent-over and out-of-shape situation is about to change. Can you not sense a shifting? A fresh wind? A new anointing? It is enveloping you, touching you, compelling you to stand up straight. If you put your hope in Jesus, he will not allow you to be ashamed. They that put their trust in God will never be shamed.

Do not give up on yourself. Do not be embarrassed because of your present circumstances; they do not decide your outcome. Praise and worship Him with expectancy while you are going through this difficult period; do not give up, stay in position and your posture of praying always. Wait with hope. Wait with expectancy.

Isaiah 40:31 (KJV) encourages:

> But they that wait upon the Lord shall renew their strength; they shall mount up with wings as eagles; they shall run and not be weary; and they shall walk and not faint.

Waiting and hoping for anything calls for patience but waiting with an attitude of gratitude takes courage and the right perspective. Keep hope alive my friend. Psalm 42:11 encourages; "Why are you cast down, O my soul? And why art thou disquieted within me? hope thou in God: for I shall yet praise him who is the health of my countenance, and my God." The book of Acts 16:16-25 also gives a scenario of Paul and Silas put in the Philippian Jail for preaching the gospel of Jesus Christ and casting a demon out of a young girl. They were told not to preach any more, then they were beaten, bruised, and chained but instead of Paul and Silas complaining…they prayed, sang, and give praises to God. During their suffering, their praise kept them with the right perspective and their conditions suddenly shifted. Their chains came loose and not only did the chains come off, but the cell doors also opened; and none of the other prisoners escaped. That same night the Jailor and his entire household were saved. Remember they did not wait for their condition to change; they praised God while in the prison and God delivered them by sending an earthquake to unlock the prison cells. God can do anything according to his word, but you must trust him in every move that you make and in all situations. Sister/brother you will not be made ashamed, you are a child of God and joint heirs with Jesus Christ.

Paul and Silas were in prison for doing good; they were in isolation because of false accusations made against them. They could have begun a pity party; (felt sorry for themselves) blame God and others for their situation but instead they chose to have a Prayer, Praise and Worship session right in jail. Your situation might not be like Paul and Silas, or it might be more dire. Let me encourage you to trust God, do not give in to those suicidal thoughts of hopelessness, worthlessness, anxiety, and most of all do not panic, God is with you, God is for you, allow him to surround you with songs of deliverance. Take note that Paul and Silas hope was in God not in man. In so doing their demeanor was one of peace and hope in God who never fails.

CHAPTER 6

Positioned for a Miracle

Now it came to pass in the days when the judges ruled, that there was a famine in the land.

—Ruth 1:1 KJV

The book of Ruth opens with a sad scene of Elimelech, who left his hometown with his wife and two sons due to a famine, but it concludes with a successful conclusion for his widow, Naomi, and her daughter-in-law, Ruth.

Naomi and her sons had gone with Elimelech from Bethlehem (the place of bread) to Moab (short of God's promises) after the "judges ruled that there was a famine in the land" (Ruth 1:1). While the family was living in Moab, Elimelech died, and his two sons, Mahlon and Chilian, married Orpah and Ruth, two women who lived in Moab. Both of Naomi's sons died leaving only her and her two daughters-in-law. Naomi realized that she was out of position, and she heard that the famine was over in Bethlehem, so she decided to go back to the place of bread.

When Naomi returned to Bethlehem with one of her daughters in law Ruth, she never in her wildest dreams imagined that she was positioning herself for the blessings of God. She had told those who welcomed her back and asked, "Now the two of them went until they came to Bethlehem. And it happened, when they came to Bethlehem, that all the city was excited because of them; and the women said, "Is this Naomi?" But she said to them, "Do not call me Naomi, call me Mara, for the Almighty has dealt very bitterly with me. I went out full, and the Lord has brought me home again empty. Why do you call me Naomi, since the Lord has testified against me, and the Almighty has afflicted me. Naomi's posture and feelings of her situation was to attribute the sovereignty of God to allow her to lose everything while out of position. Although the name of God was not mentioned or written in the book of Ruth, yet we find his mercy, love, hand, and sovereignty on every page.

We can get bent over (bitter) and out of shape during our times of famine and leave the blessed place because we feel we have been overlooked, talked about, ostracized, criticized, and we feel that God wants us to move on, but God in his infinite mercy will allow us to get back in position as he did with Naomi. Have you left Bethlehem (House of Bread- Hebrew meaning)? Have you given up and left the blessed place due to a famine that was beyond your control? Acknowledge your mistake; and like the Prodigal Son in Saint Luke 15:11-32, arise and go back home Father God awaits your return without judgment or partiality. Job's posture and perspective when he lost everything; including his health and his wife admonished him to 'curse God and die' was also like Naomi, he acknowledged the sovereignty of God by saying: "What? Shall we receive good at the hand of God, and shall we not receive evil?? (Job 2:10b). Job positioned himself to receive double for his trouble by praying for his friends who accused him of sinning against God.

You may have been abused physically, verbally, sexually, or psychologically and have carried that terrible secret for years and your view and trust of people might have become tainted and dimmed by the abuse you have suffered. You might be hurting because of your spouse's infidelity. You may be in a bent-over position carrying the load of unresolved issues, and you feel that you want to check out. Suicidal thoughts have been troubling you, and you want to give up, but I encourage you to stay in the position of prayer. Do not lose your position of praise even when you do not feel like it. Open your mouth and give God praise. He knows where you are; he hears your cry, and he is with you now. You may not feel him, but you are not alone; he has you. He sees and understands your every groan. Stay in the position of expectancy. Remember that God's grace— unmerited divine aid given for regeneration or sanctification according to *Merriam Webster's*—is sufficient.

Bartimaeus, a blind man in Jericho (Mark 10:46–52 NIV), had heard that Jesus was passing by, and he waited expectantly at the entrance for him. The crowd was large, so he called out, "Jesus, son of David, have mercy on me!" The crowd tried to shut him up. People told him that Jesus was too busy and did not have time for him or that his blindness was too far gone and there was no help for him. Regardless, Bartimaeus did not give up. His years of blindness would finally end if he could only get Jesus's attention. So, he cried out louder and more persistently; his cry became one of desperation. This blind man had been bent over for far too long, and no one was going to stop him. Today was his day!

Are you in position? Are you desperate? Do you need a miracle? A miracle is an effect or extraordinary event in the physical world that surpasses all known human or natural powers and is ascribed to a supernatural cause. You may be in a desperate situation that only God can fix. Do you really need a miracle? A miracle comes by faith in God alone. Human intellect cannot produce miracles, but God can.

This blind man needed a miracle that the psychics could not predict, and the doctors could not cure, and when you need a miracle or a breakthrough that badly, you will do anything to get Jesus's attention. This man refused to be silent any longer. He decided to cry out even louder. You may have been carrying around silent pain. Beloved, cry out to Jesus, and seek help from trusted counselors. Do not live another day, another moment in silence; it is your day to get his attention. This is your opportunity to receive that for which you have been waiting. It is your time for a supernatural breakthrough. Tell the enemy, "You had me silent long enough, and enough is enough!"

The enemy does not want to see you delivered, but it is your time, so let no one and nothing stop you. Your faith has placed you in line for a supernatural turnaround. You were not there when Jesus went into Jericho, you did not make it to the big revival, but you are now in position, and you have found your voice. Cry out, "Jesus! Have mercy on me! Save me, deliver me, help me, and set me free." Others might want to silence you, to stop your voice, to shut you down, to stop your praise, but let your praise flow from the inside out. There is a shout that wants to break loose; let it out now in Jesus' name. Throw your garment of heaviness aside and put on the garment of praise. Your sight is back, your joy is back, and your pain is gone. You are free to follow Jesus and free to tell others about the love of God. He is calling you to come to him and cast your cares on him. He is all you need.

Prayer—A Posture for the Supernatural

> Then Elijah said to Ahab, "Go to get something to eat and drink, for I hear a mighty rainstorm coming!" So, Ahab went to eat and drink, but Elijah climbed to the top of Mount Carmel and bowed low to the ground and prayed with his face between his knees. Then he said to his servant and look out toward the sea." The servant went and looked, then returned to Elijah and said, "I didn't see anything." Seven times Elijah told him to go and look. Finally, the seventh time, his servant told him, "I saw a little cloud about the size of a man's hand rising from the sea." (1 Kings 18:41–44 NLT)

While waiting for your healing or your situation to change, stay in the posture of persistent prayer, expectancy, and praise. The bent over woman waited for eighteen years, and the man who lay at the pool of Bethesda waited for thirty-eight years in the position of expectation and waiting. Once you realize that the condition that you are in is not permanent, you are ready for the miraculous to take place in your life.

Like Naomi, you may have come out of position due to circumstances beyond your control; you may think that all is lost, but I encourage you to go back to that place of personal devotion, find that secret place where you and God used to have intimate conversations, and allow yourself to be immersed in his love and compassion. He is waiting for you.

CHAPTER 7

Stand Up and Praise

And he laid *His* hands on her: and immediately she was made straight, and glorified (praised) God.

Luke 13:13 KJ/NKJV

The word *stand* is not a passive instruction but a verb, an action word, which promotes a rising, taking a position.

Acts 3:2-12 tell us that one day at about three in the afternoon, Peter and John were on their way to the Temple for the hour of prayer. They encountered a lame man who was carried and placed daily at the gate named Beautiful Gate of the Temple to ask Alms from those going in the temple. When he asked Peter and John to give him something, Peter tool the lame man "Look at us...silver and gold we do not have, but what I have I give unto you. In the name of Jesus Christ of Nazareth rise and walk. My brother/sister, that lame man was expecting money, but money nor a handout could have purchased what he received that day. Acts 3: went on to tell us that Peter took him by the right hand and raised him up and immediately his feet and ankles received strength and he leaped up, stood on his feet, walking with them into the Temple, leaping and praising God. The lame man responded to the word of faith, begin to believe God for his healing, stood up and start praising God. This man was born lame, so he had no reference point on how to walk, yet he did. Do not wait until what you were believing for come to past, praise now! What is your response to the word of faith that you are reading, that has been spoken over your life? Stand up, leap, walk and start praising God.

The bent-over woman had struggled for eighteen years, but her time, her season, had shifted on that Sabbath day. Ecclesiastes 3 (NIV) states, "There is a time for everything, and a season for every activity under the heavens." Jesus called her to the front, from a place of anonymity to a place of prominence. He called her from a place of shame and isolation to a place of unapologetic praise. "He laid His hand on her." Just to think of God's hands touching us should be a wonderful reason to glorify him.

When Jesus called this woman to the front from among all the others in the house that day, that was a miracle. God knows exactly where we are. I wondered whether that was Jesus's first time at that synagogue; if it was not, why was she not healed before? Was she absent the times before? But my thoughts led me to Psalm 31:15 (NIV): "My times are in your hand." When it is your time, nothing or no one can hinder the move of God in your life.

God is never casual about what he does for his people and for those who trust him; everything he does is intentional. Isaiah 46:10 says, "I make known the end from the beginning, from ancient times, what is still to come. I say, 'My purpose will stand, and I will do as I please.'"

Jesus helped this bent-over woman in ways as mentioned in Luke 13:10–17 (NKJV).

1. **He Taught the Word of God (v. 10)**

"For the word of God is alive and active. Sharper than any double-edged sword, it penetrates even to the dividing soul and spirit, joints, and marrow; it judges the thoughts and attitudes of the heart" (Luke 4:12 NIV). As Jesus taught the Word, this woman's faith reached a level of receiving complete healing. Romans 10:17 states, "So then faith cometh by hearing and hearing the word of God." The Word of God will set you free.

2. **Jesus Saw Her (v. 12)**

He not only saw her disability; he also saw perseverance, he saw her heart, her deepest desire, he saw her longing to be set free from her infirmity and he also saw her faith. God alone discerns the intent and the thoughts of the heart of every human being. Psalm 139 acknowledges that God is omnipresent; he is everywhere even in the most secret places, and He knows our thoughts. He saw her future and he saw her potential. He saw the liberated woman; he saw you and me. He saw the finished product. Isaiah 46:10 says: "I make known the end from the beginning, from ancient times, what is still to come. I say, 'My purpose will stand, and I will do all that I please,'

3. **Jesus Called Her (v. 12)**

Jesus called her forward and confronted the root of her bent-over issues and declared healing of what had had her bound for eighteen years: "Woman you are set free from your infirmity." He called her from obscurity. He called her and spoke to her insecurities due to her condition. What a compassionate and loving Savior. He heals all our diseases and binds up the broken spirit and pours the balm of Gilead on the wounded. He is calling YOU!

4. **He Laid His Hand on Her (v. 13)**

Wow! Why would Jesus lay his hand on her after he had declared her healed? I surmised that every now and again, we need to feel the literal hands of the Savior on and in our lives. His touch was one of affirmation and approval to be all that she was created to become. Jesus knew that this woman craved the human touch, but a God kind of touch was necessary. A touch of compassion, a touch of reassurance that you can do it. Yes, you can get up from that affliction, you can stand up.

When Jesus places his hand on you my brother/sister, your life will never be the same. Luke 13:13 (NIV) puts it this way: "And immediately she straightened up." She responded to the touch of Jesus by straightening up, and she praised God. When God does anything for us, our response should be one of adoration and exuberant praise. This woman's praise was undignified and unorthodox and disrupted the otherwise normal routine on that Sabbath day.

5. **Jesus Defended Her Legal Rights to Be Heal (vv. 15–16)**

She was a daughter of Abraham and had earned the right to be healed because of her unwavering faith after all those years of having this infirmity. Not everyone wants you to be free. The leaders of the synagogue were outraged that Jesus had the audacity to heal on the Sabbath day. They said: "There are six days for work; therefore, come and be healed on those days, not on the Sabbath Day." Brother/sister, healing is available for all in the atonement of Christ's death on the cross for those who receive by faith no matter what hour of the day or day of the week it is. Isaiah 53:5 (KJV) declares, "But he was wounded for our transgressions, he was bruised for our iniquities; the chastisement of our peace was upon him, and with his stripes we are healed." He defended this woman's rights to be healed by confronting their hypocrisy. "You hypocrites! Doesn't each of you on the Sabbath untie your ox or donkey from the stall and lead it out to give it water? Then should not this woman, a daughter, whom Satan has kept bound for eighteen long years, be set free on the Sabbath day from what bound her?" Luke 13:15-16(NIV). Jesus is our defender, our High Priest, and our Intercessor.

If you are waiting and believing God for anything, trust him and receive his Word. He sees you, so answer his call to come forth and stand up, feel his touch, and praise him. You have been enslaved in that situation, with that disease long enough. You are free in Jesus' name.

Conclusion

Life sometimes might seem unfair, and you may have received blows that left you bent over. You have questioned and even prayed and asked, "Why me?" Things and situations seem hopeless, and you do not want to go on, but let me encourage you, give up and do not give in to the temptation to whine and complain. God has not forgotten you. He knows your name; he has the hairs on your head numbered. God knew you before you were formed in your mother's womb. Jeremiah 1:5 (NIV) affirms that your birth was not an accident or an afterthought no matter what the circumstances of your birth was; God declared, "Before I formed you in the womb I knew you, before you were born, I set you apart; I appointed you as a prophet to the nations."

Jeremiah knew exactly how you and I may feel at times—inadequate, worthless, socially unacceptable, and bent over. But God knows our worth and that we are indeed special. Just as he reassured Jeremiah, he reassures and affirms your purpose for living. God calls you to be effective; his hands are on you, so stand up straight and praise the God who has not forgotten you. Jesus went that Sabbath day just for that one woman who was bent- over for eighteen years, and he has come just for you. You do not have to stay in the shape that you are in; the Potter wants to put you back together again. Stand up and declare that "I am free my infirmity. You are free to stand tall and shout his praises loud and clear.

You are in the right place. You have waited long enough; he has come in answer to your silent tears and deepest groanings. He has responded to your persistent faith and earnest expectations that something greater was coming. All eyes are on him because he has called you out from the back to the front; he has touched you, and your life will never be that same. Stand up straight!

About the Author

Patricia Clarke Rolle, a devout Christian, speaks to the inner pain every person experiences at different stages of their lives with her writing, urging her readers to seek light and love by turning to God. Bent but Not Broken is her first book.

I was born and raised in the beautiful Nation of The Bahamas and I live in Nassau, Bahamas

I have been in Ministry for about 45 years: 20 years in evangelism (Traveled extensively throughout the Bahama Islands, USA, Central America, Dominican Republic, Turks & Caicos Islands, the Holy Land (Israel) and currently I am serving as Senior Pastor of Cornerstone Church of God (22 years).

I have served in various Ministries in the local church (Southland Church of God) including:

1. Sunday School
2. Family Training Director
3. Innercircle President(a mentoring program for young women(18-25)
4. Bus Driver
5. Church Secretary
6. Marriage Ministry President(along with my husband)
7. National Evangelist (Church of God Bahamas)

Education:

Diploma in Early Childhood(College of The Bahamas (UB)
Certificate in Painting and Decoration (Bahamas Vocation Technical Institute)
Diploma in Secretarially Science (Betz School of Business, Hialeah, Florida
An Associate of Science Degree in Radio and Television Broadcasting (Miami
    Dade Community College
A Licensed Ordained Minister in the Church of God
A Certified Chaplain
A Certificate in Leadership
A Justice of the Peace

Martial Status

Married
four adult children.

Work

Retired from the Ministry of Health/Department of Public Health as Clinic
Administrator, having served for over 20 years.

Hobbies:

Love to read
Love to travel and experience the joy of meeting new people
An avid Public Speaker

Printed in the United States
by Baker & Taylor Publisher Services